S. WENCESLAVS MARTYR
primus Rex Bohemiæ

The illustrations are from the album "Dějiny české" by Antonín Machek, from the book "Diadochus" by Bartoloměj Paprocký z Hlohol and from old Czech prints from the XVIIth–XIXth centuries.

The cover painting of Saint Wenceslas is by Josef Mánes.

The publisher thanks all those who contributed with advice and help, or by loans, towards collecting the rare illustrations.

Eduard Petiška

The Lives of St. Wenceslas,

St. Ludmila and St. Adalbert

MARTIN

ISBN 80-900129-8-1

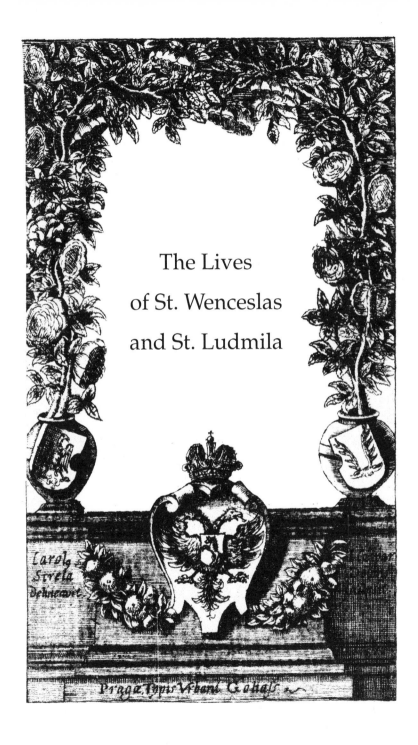

The Lives

of St. Wenceslas

and St. Ludmila

VERA EFFIGIES
S. WENCESLAI Mart:
Patroni Boëmiæ Rni
Qui ætatis. 23 Å:
vero Salutis 929
à Fratre Boles-
lao necat, est.

Wlastni Obraz
S. Waczlawa Muž:
Patrona Kralowst:
Czeskeho. kterýzto
wieku sweho. w. 23.
a Letha Panie 929.
od Bratra Boleslawa
Zamordowan byl.

It remains to cross the threshold that divides
darkness of legend from dusk of history.
In the region where the Czech rivers embrace,
two mighty families embraced in their children.
But history has time, only legend hastens,
arriving at the place before the clouds,
and shining before the light awakens.

A SON AND A DAUGHTER

Once long ago, during the reign of Prince Nezamysl, and old legend says, Pšov castle was founded on a high hill. And it was a place with an unusually beautiful view over the countryside, in which Říp hill raised its rounded, thoughtful forehead above the level of the meadow and forests. And three waters flowed round the hill bearing Pšov castle. The river Elbe, hurrying from the east of the sun, here accepted the river Vltava, hurrying from the south, from Prague, Vyšehrad and Levý Hradec, and the third water at the foot of the hill was a stream whose waters seldom froze.

Those who built Pšov castle knew very well that the height of the hill was a defence against the enemy and that rivers are the mother of life. And from those days men lived in Pšov who administered the tribe of the Pšovans. The territory of this tribe reached along the Elbe and up to the north and neighboured on the Bohemian princedom on the left bank of the Elbe and on Litoměřice to the west and the territory of the Croats to the east. During the reign of Prince Hostivít the wise and just Slavibor lived in Pšov castle. He had the castle refortified and made it into a strong, invulnerable seat.

Slavibor was one of those governors of the people who see to their good. He founded new villages and farmsteads, he had forests burnt and increased the fertile land. Legend tells that he also had Houska castle built on a tall sandstone cliff. Not long after the castle was ready and people moved into it, a very strange thing happened. In the forest near Houska castle the cliff burst open, and spirits who harmed both people and crops came out of the hole into the woods. At night or when it was misty they took on the most terrifying likenesses, wandered around the castle and frightened anyone who was on the road out of their lives. These weird phenomena made people afraid to leave the castle, and when the rampaging of these evil spirits did not cease, they deserted the castle altogether, possessed by fear of a threatening danger. Houska castle became dilapidated. Only many centuries later the Lords of Dubé built a new castle in its place.

The wife of Prince Hostivít bore a son and the prince invited the leaders of friendly tribes from near and far to a celebration. One of the guests was Slavibor of Pšov, and the festivities lasted three days and three nights. The prince's son was given the name of Bořivoj. The halls of Vyšehrad rang with talk and laughter, mead trickled over chins and carefree joy reigned. Not one of those who went to look at the new-born child dreamt that with Bořivoj a new age had been born, that would sweep away the old order that the people of this country had been used to for long centuries. But Bořivoj was still at the beginning of his life. He slept, and in his sleep he clenched his pink little fist. And the old men foretold that he would grow into a gallant warrior who relied on the strength of his fists. But which of those old men could guess whom that childish fist would grow to fight?

S. LUDMILLA.

Slavibor too was happy at the sight of the child. He was linked to Hostivít by friendship and Hostivít paid him the honours due to the head of a friendly tribe. Before Slavibor bade farewell to Vyšehrad he asked Hostivít to visit him in Pšov castle.

As soon as spring gave its hand to summer Hostivít rode out with his company to visit the tribal castle of the Pšovans. From the far distance he already saw a mighty hill over the river with a castle at its summit. He loudly praised the position of Slavibor's castle. Slavibor's servants rode out to meet the prince and showed him the ford across the Elbe, leading him and his people through the shallow water to the other bank.

The lord of Pšov welcomed Prince Hostivít with great acclaim and stateliness. They feasted and drank together and after the feast Slavibor showed Hostivít over the castle. Hostivít looked out from the battlements and there his princedom stretched before him beyond the Elbe like a precious picture wrought of silver and gold, set with precious stones of green and sky-blue, and among the sparkle and glitter, the sharp lights and delicious shadows, lay Říp hill, that helmet inherited from his ancestors. Hostivít gazed enchanted at his lands. When he lived in the midst of them they did not seem so beautiful as now, when he had crossed their borders and looked on them from afar. When at last he tore his eyes from the picture that had made his heart beat faster, he said to Slavibor of Pšov:

"Dear friend, if Vyšehrad had such a position as this, not only Bohemian princes would have their seat there, but the immortal gods themselves."

For four days Hostivít and his company lived as guests at Pšov castle, and after four days the time came to say farewell. Slavibor called his servants and with them he accompanied the Bohemian prince on horseback.

It happened that at that time the Elbe had gleaned a great deal of water from the mountains and tributaries, and treacherous whirlpools had hollowed out holes in places that had formerly been passable. The horsemen

entered the water and were swept away by the strong current and the depths. Terrified horses and people floated helplessly down the river. Hostivít lost his horse from beneath him and only with great effort, by swimming his hardest, did he reach the opposite bank. Slavibor too lost his horse, and almost lost his life. Several of the servants from both companies found death in the waters. Those who survived that unhappy river crossing found shelter in a nearby village. Only after resting and with fresh horses Prince Hostivít and Slavibor made for Vyšehrad. The ill luck that they had survived together brought the two rulers still closer together.

After a time Hostivít's enemies in the Bílinský region rose against him, and enemies from the Kouřim region pestered him too. Slavibor never deserted Prince Hostivít and the swords and arrows of the Pšovans were always on the side of the Czechs. So the friendship between the two tribes was strengthened by their fight against a common enemy. Hostivít and Slavibor came out of the battles as victors, as they had once come out of the fierce current of the flooded river.

In Pšov castle a daughter was born to Slavibor's wife. They named her Ludmila. Slavibor invited guests from near and far to celebrate the birth of his daughter. In the first place his friend, the Bohemian Prince Hostivít.

The body of the night lay over the whole landscape with the rivers and Říp hill, but the banqueting hall in Pšov was brightly lit. Gleeful talk and laughter winged their way round the timbered walls. Only in the chamber where the little girl slept was there silence. Three Fates in snow-white robes met at her cradle. The were weaving the child the thread of life and measuring it.

The first Fate said:

"Your destiny, Ludmila, will be linked with the destiny of the boy who lives in the castle over the Vltava river. The name of the boy is Bořivoj."

The second Fate said:

"Your future, Ludmila, is hidden in your name. You will love your people, and your people will love you."

Vyšehrad

The third Fate said:

"You will die a sad death, Ludmila, but your memory will live a joyous life."

The three white figures of the Fates dissolved into the darkness and the days and years that followed began to fulfil Ludmila's and Bořivoj's destiny.

When one day you pass through Moravian land,
it may hap that you'll step upon some grass-grown turf
beneath which slumber ruins of castle or church
of an ancient empire.
You will not know what it is you tread on,
your thoughts deeply occupied with your own cares and joys.
Then flying high over the field a lark will sing —
that is the song of the great empire,
a raven will fall heavily on the furrow —
that is the song of the great empire.
The living tell legends of the long since dead
and the dead can only listen.

A GREAT SLAV EMPIRE

Over a thousand years ago a thick forest grew on the eastern borders of the Czech land. Trees and thickets climbed over the slopes, covering the hills and hiding within their green shade wild animals, boulders, rushing streams and treacherous marshes. Several paths led through the forest, linking Czech land with Moravian, yet a wayfarer unfamiliar with the country would often lose his way. In a short time the path became overgrown, greenery flowed over the ways cut by man.

And there were times when the wild animals fled into the depths of the forest and the birds rose screeching from the branches. This was when a foreign army tramped along the path, returning from a campaign in Moravia across Czech land to Germany. It was always a difficult journey, marked by hardships and heavy losses. The enemy was never sure in which thicket a bow-string was just being pulled, from which slope a boulder would crash down to bring him destruction. So that often the foreign warriors' only booty was death.

The House of the Přemyslides ruled at that time in the very heart of Bohemia. In Moravia the rulers were from the tribe of Prince Mojmír. Mojmír united the Slav tribes living in Moravia and laid the foundations for a great Slav empire. And it is said that a famous prince of Mojmír's family, Rostislav, settled in an especially powerful castle on the river Morava, possibly where the town called Staré Město now stands. That powerful castle was named Velehrad.

A small group of Christian priests was wandering around the Slav villages and castles in those days. They came from the west and were attempting to convert the heathen Slavs to the Christian faith. Some of these priests could only speak the Slav language very poorly, others could speak passably well, but all of them mainly had in mind the interests and gain of the foreign sovereign who had sent them from the west. As soon as they opened their mouths the native people recognized that the language of these new arrivals was the language of the enemy. The sign of the cross, which they brought with them, frightened the local gods. The foreigners raised the cross in front of them as a warrior raises his sword before he strikes. The eyes and the ears of old men and women, the blind and the deaf, were suddenly opened, and their eyes were filled with a vision of the destruction of the old days and their mouths were full of prophesies of evil.

Then the mighty Moravian Prince Rostislav, lord of his subjects, summoned his people to Velehrad and held council with them. He was not afraid of the new Christian religion, but he was afraid of the cross that came from Germany. The German cross meant danger to the independence of the Moravian land. The prince and the councillors and the people consulted together and they decided to turn to the east, from where the sun rises and with it hope. They fitted out a deputation and sent it to the distant city of Constantinople, where the Byzantine Emperor Michael reigned. And the Emperor Michael rejoiced in the new friendship with the mighty Moravian prince, feasted the deputation and fulfilled their requests. He sent to Moravia teachers of the Christian religion who spoke the Slav language and served their God alone, not the German emperor. And so there came from the east, where the sun rises and with it hope, two brothers — Constantine, also called Cyril, and Methodius. They came to Velehrad with their retinue, bearing with them the relics of St. Clement and gifts from the Emperor Michael, including that most precious gift of all: the Glagolitic script. Constantine, who was learned in languages, had composed this script for the Slavs. Constantine also translated the essential parts of the Christian religious service into Old Slavonic and wrote it in his own lettering, so that the local people might understand it.

When Constantine's and Methodius's train approached the gates of Velehrad, Prince Rostislav came to meet them together with his company, which included Svatopluk, a kinsman of Rostislav's. All of them greeted the two ambassadors of the Christian faith with great pomp and dignity.

Constantine was the youngest of seven children and Methodius was the oldest. Constantine was full of fire and he sparked the enthusiasm of those who were near him. Methodius was full of quiet light. Constantine loved learning and lofty dreams, while Methodius tended towards godly contemplation and cloistered seclusion. Now both of them grappled with their new tasks, each in his own way.

The Moravians regarded their doings with both trust and mistrust. To some it seemed that the cross brought from the east spread its crossbeam like the wings of a peaceful dove. But others could not cease to see it as a sword aimed at the heart of the old heathen beliefs. Some accepted the new doctrine, others resisted it stubbornly with clenched fist.

Christianity began to spread from Velehrad over the whole country, supported by the prince and by his councillors. Constantine and Methodius soon had enough disciples who could preach to the people understandably in the Slav language.

The time had come for Christian law and the heathen gods were swept into the fire, the heathen temples were destroyed and the heathen priests became fugitives, hiding in the forests to avoid imprisonment.

Constantine wrote a code of laws for the people, which imposed punishment for heathens. The new laws stated that every village where sacrifices were made to the heathen gods was to pass to the ownership of the church. If a village lord was devoted to heathen customs, he and his fortune were to be sold and the profit from the sale given to the poor.

Light and comfort came from Velehrad for some, for others anxiety.

Constantine and Methodius preached to the people of the Christian God, who is love, and he who resides in love resides in God and God in him. And the seed of their words fell on rock. Violence and guile did not cease to rule even in the princely family, which had accepted Christianity.

Svatopluk, Prince Rostislav's nephew, gave precedence to his personal good before family and language ties. He subjected himself and his lands to Carloman, son of the German king. Rostislav's power was diminished by Svatopluk's land and the prince considered his nephew's deed treachery that called for retribution. And the only retribution for such treachery was death. The prince invited Svatopluk to Velehrad and Svatopluk accepted the invitation as one free prince accepts an invitation from another. He sat down to table with Rostislav at feasts and was not discomforted by the displeasure written in the princely frown. The prince frowned and waited. He had himself chosen the moment when the hired assassins were to strangle Svatopluk. And it is said that the Christian God, who had chosen the way of victory for Svatopluk and not the way of destruction, warned his protégé in time. Svatopluk got up before the appointed moment, before the assassins entered the hall, and went out under the pretext that he was going to look at the falcons. A hunt was going to start soon and horses were waiting for their riders in front of the palace. Svatopluk leapt up onto one of the horses standing ready and called to those of his company who were near to follow him. The band of horsemen left Velehrad with Svatopluk, and before the prince was told what had happened Svatopluk had the lead.

Rostislav was seized with wrath, and he obeyed its evil advice. He rode forth with a detachment of those faithful to him, following Svatopluk's tracks, still fresh in the wet grass. The tracks led to Svatopluk's estate. Rostislav was determined to follow Svatopluk even as far as his castle. But it happened that the trap that Rostislav had laid for his nephew at the feast turned against him. In a bend in the forest road the prince and his escort were ambushed by Svatopluk and his men and, after a short fight, he was dragged from his horse and led in chains to Svatopluk's castle. From there he set out on a sad journey to Bavaria, to the court of judgment of the German king, with whom Svatopluk had concluded an alliance. Betrayal begot betrayal and was devoured by betrayal.

The German king then summoned his assembly and this assembly condemned Prince Rostislav to death for opposition to the German king. But the king granted him mercy. A mercy more cruel than death. He ordered that Rostislav be blinded and imprisoned in a monastery, where he disappeared as into the deepest grave.

Carloman marched on Rostislav's territory with Svatopluk, plundering it and taking booty. He even carried off Rostislav's splendid treasure. He installed Svatopluk as ruler. At last Svatopluk reigned from Rostislav's castle, at last his wish was fulfilled.

But the favour of kings is as inconstant as the shadow of a grass. The slightest breeze will blow it the opposite way. Svatopluk soon fell into disfavour with Carloman, though once he had voluntarily become his subject. He was thrown into prison and two German lords were appointed instead of him to govern the Moravian land.

But the Moravian Slavs revolted and refused to obey the foreigners. They elected a new prince from Mojmír's family, for they supposed that Svatopluk had died in captivity. The new prince was named Slavomar and it was again Rostislav's castle that became his seat. A minor war undermined the power of the two German governors and the territory over which Slavomar ruled increased.

Carloman, surprised by the Moravian resistance, began to prepare for war. He ordered that Svatopluk be brought from prison and showered him with royal gifts. He knew Svatopluk's longing to return to his native land and he knew his ambition. He gained a promise from Svatopluk that he would return to Moravia at the head of Carloman's army. Svatopluk did ride out with Carloman's soldiers against Slavomar, but he bore one single thought in his heart — to revenge himself on Carloman for his imprisonment and humiliation.

When the Bavarian army reached Rostislav's old castle Svatopluk entered its gates alone, as if he wanted to negotiate with Slavomar. And while the army built a camp beneath the castle and waited, expecting that Slavomar would surrender to their superior numbers without a fight, Svatopluk agreed with Slavomar on how to gain victory over the foreigners.

Like the onslaught of a storm the Slav warriors hurled themselves on the Bavarian camp from all sides. The foreign soldiers were so taken by surprise that they had not even time to raise their weapons. Unprecedented spoils and countless prisoners fell into the hands of the Moravian Slavs. The two German governors chosen to rule the country were killed.

The German king was visited by a great grief when he

heard of the defeat of his son's army. Svatopluk again became the ruler of his land.

The time of Svatopluk's rule meant a time of more and more battles, a time rich in the glory of war, and Svatopluk's power grew. Once again Rostislav's ancient castle became the centre of a great Moravian empire.

Svatopluk was called Svatopluk the Great, and he was called king. He united under his rule the extensive territory of Moravia, part of Austria, Slovakia and the territory along the rivers Oder and Vistula. Even the land of Bohemia and the Polabian Sorbs to the north of Bohemia, and the Slavs in the Tisza valley came under Svatopluk's rule. So over a thousand years ago a mighty state arose, in which Czechs, Moravians and Slovaks had their common home.

The years passed by and Constantine's and Methodius's work bore fruit. Their successes found disfavour with the German priests. The brothers were accused before the Pope of serving mass in the Slav language and not in Latin as was the custom. Constantine and Methodius had to go to Rome to defend their teaching. The Pope accepted from Constantine's hand a translation of liturgical books and, as a sign that he recognized them, he laid them on the altar in the Roman cathedral. It seemed that the brothers had triumphed over the German bishops, who envied them the wide territories of the Moravian empire. But joy in victory was brief. Constantine never returned to Velehrad. He died in Rome. And further troubles awaited Methodius. When he returned to Moravia as archbishop he was captured by the German priests, tormented, beaten and tortured in the snow in cruel cold and then thrown into prison. Only when there was a new Pope did he succeed in freeing Archbishop Methodius.

At the time when Methodius had again taken over the administration of Christian affairs in Velehrad the Czech Prince Bořivoj visited Velehrad. When Svatopluk entered the banqueting hall with Bořivoj and the nobles, Svatopluk and the nobles sat at table and Bořivoj was assigned a place on the floor.

Bořivoj hesitated and turned to Svatopluk: "I cannot understand," he said, "why I should sit on the floor while you and your nobles feast at the table."

"Such is the heathen and such the Christian manner," Svatopluk replied. "Heathens feast on the floor and it is fitting that Christians should feast in the Christian manner."

Bořivoj considered this and asked to be instructed in the Christian faith. Methodius himself talked to him at length about the Christian God, who is one and invisible. Methodius's kind words moved Prince Bořivoj to call his company and have them taught by Methodius's disciples about the new faith. The prince and his company then fasted and had themselves baptized. So Bořivoj had come to Velehrad as a heathen and he left as a Christian with a Christian retinue. Svatopluk the Great gave him gifts and sent the priest Kaich with him, so that he could preach the new faith in Bohemia. Kaich took with him the relics of St. Clement.

Prince Bořivoj settled the priest in Levý Hradec and there together they founded the church of St. Clement, the first Christian church in Bohemia.

But the people clung to their heathen customs and the old ways and could not reconcile themselves with the new laws. The heathen priests' anger turned against Bořivoj and the prince had to save himself by escaping to Svatopluk in Moravia.

After some time messengers came from Bohemia begging Prince Bořivoj to return and not desert his people. Only then did Bořivoj go back to Bohemia.

It is said that Svatopluk was of a violent nature and led the wild life of a warrior. His amusements were hunting and riotous feasting. None of this was compatible with the teachings of Methodius. Svatopluk found Christianity good for governing his subjects, but he had little taste for Christianity governing him. Dispute followed dispute and quarrel followed quarrel, till the relationship between the archbishop and the Moravian ruler was like an incessant, bitter war.

Bořivoj

One holy day in summer, when the Velehrad church was filling with believers and the bells pealed far and wide across the country, Svatopluk was engaged in hunting beyond the river. Archbishop Methodius was already enrobed for high mass, but Svatopluk did not return. Methodius had two choices: either to prefer his god and not wait till Svatopluk came, or to prefer his prince and let God wait. He decided to prefer God and started to celebrate the mass.

In the middle of the service shouting and noise could be heard in front of the church, neighing horses, pounding hoofs and the notes of a hunting horn. The church door flew open and an enraged Svatopluk ran in, his spear raised, as if it was not the archbishop standing before him on the altar steps, but a wild animal. The dogs that accompanied the prince on his hunts burst into the church behind him and, made boisterous by the recent chase, desecrated the calm and peace of the service with their barking.

"Halt!" Methodius called to Svatopluk.

But Svatopluk ran up to the altar and drew back his spear to strike.

"Hold hard!" cried Methodius and raised his right hand against Svatopluk. This movement reminded Svatopluk of the boundary between earthly estates, where he was the master, and unearthly ones looked after by Methodius. He let his spear fall, turned and left the church, surrounded by his favourite dogs. Svatopluk never forgave Methodius that encounter before the eyes of the people.

Svatopluk the Great liked to listen to the western priests, who blackened Methodius's name and toadied to Svatopluk. The western priests did not scold Svatopluk and tried to win over his harsh character by gentleness and compliance.

From that moment Methodius did not see a single peaceful day and the number of his enemies multiplied. But the restless days of his life were soon ended by death.

After the death of Methodius his successor, Gorazd,

had to leave the country. All those whom Methodius had taught were first cruelly and ignominiously imprisoned and then banished. Most of them found their way to the land of Bulgaria, where they deserve merit for the blossoming of Slav literature.

Svatopluk was a mighty ruler, apparently strong and invincible. But inwardly he was racked with fears for the fate of his empire. He reflected on how to divide his property amongst his sons, so that what he had conquered should not disintegrate in battle and the chaos of war.

He had his three sons called and allocated to each a share of his empire, and he appointed the oldest the supreme ruler. The two younger brothers were to obey him. Then he commanded a servant to bring three sticks. He tied them firmly together and handed them to his oldest son.

"Try to break the sticks," he said.

The oldest son grasped the bound sticks, tried to break them, but could not.

Svatopluk passed the sticks to his second son.

"You try and break them," he said.

The second son tried to break the sticks and could not.

Finally Svatopluk gave them to the youngest son.

Not even he could break the sticks.

Then Svatopluk untied the sticks and gave one to each son. Now they broke the sticks easily.

"Never forget this moment," said Svatopluk, "and act on my advice. So long as all three of you stand together in harmony and love, no enemy will overcome you. If you part in quarrels and stand one against the other you will lose the strength you had so long as you were united. The enemy will break each one of you separately and will destroy the whole empire."

And when he had left his empire to his sons it is said that he departed from the army camp unobserved at night. He disappeared from the midst of his soldiers. Only after a lapse of time the story went round that he had gone into a thick forest where, in a hidden place, he had killed his horse and buried his sword and princely robe. At dawn he reached the dwelling of some hermits who had once built a church in that forest with his support. They did not recognize who had come to them. Svatopluk clothed himself in hermit's garb.

He is said to have lived there with the hermits unrecognized for some time, only disclosing to them who he was in the hour of his death.

The Great Moravian Empire did not escape the fate that Svatopluk had feared. His sons quarrelled with one another. The Czechs and the Polabian Sorbs took advantage of this discord and broke away from the empire, which later began to crumble altogether. A part of Great Moravia, today Slovakia, was occupied by the Hungarians and Moravia was governed by the Czech house of the Přemyslides.

The fame of the ancient mighty Slav empire was forgotten. Grass grew on the hilltops where once the castles and stone churches of Greater Moravia stood. Trees struck root in their aged earthen walls and tumbled ramparts. The name Velehrad was given to a monastery that was built several centuries later. By then the famous, mighty and invulnerable castle of Prince Rostislav was all but forgotten, even the place where it stood.

What the sword had conquered was lost. But what was conquered in those days by the human spirit, what was conquered by ingenuity and skill, has been brought down to us on the waves of ages, to our century.

The heathen gods and idols beat a retreat,
they went away to woodland thickets, hid themselves in wells,
fire consumed them, water swept them away,
in their place the Christian God moved into our country,
he was foreign and no one could see him
and he spoke through the mouths of his priests
of the love of man for man.
And as time passed
the heathen killed the Christians
and the Christians the heathen
and when there were no more heathen
the Christians killed Christians
for someone's love
of old, dead things
such as plunder and power.

THE RETREAT OF THE OLD GODS

Bohemia was ruled by Prince Bořivoj. Long ago he had taken Ludmila, Slavibor's daughter, from Pšov castle, to be his wife. Thus the first part of the Fate's prophesy was fulfilled. Ludmila was beautiful and winsome, and the people loved her for her goodness. And so the second part of the prophesy was fulfilled. And merciless time prepared the third part. In those years Archbishop Methodius died in Velehrad, and his adherents and disciples incurred Svatopluk's displeasure. They fled from Moravia and some of them came to Bohemia to Prince Bořivoj. Bořivoj received them kindly and their arrival encouraged the religious services held in the Slav language. Both Bořivoj and Ludmila were dedicated to the new Christian religion. And they had their sons, Spytihněv and Vratislav, christened. Bořivoj and Ludmila were said to be happiest when they sought seclusion in the quiet of Tetín castle. Here the old gods had been worshipped for long ages, and now the worship of the new God found a home there.

There were many heathen idols in the Tetín woods. The local people remembered Krok's famous daughter, Teta, who had taught them to honour nymphs and woodland spirits and spring-water and fire. With Bořivoj's arrival a new order reigned. He commanded that the idols be cut down in the name of the one and only invisible Christian God. And a feud broke out between those who loved the old customs and the old faith, and those who loved the new faith. And there were many who hesitated, not declaring their faith much. They waited to see which side power and victory inclined to, so that they could join the stronger. At that time it was not clear in Bohemia who would win the struggle. The heathen priests fled from the new faith into the forest and their faithful followed them there.

Legend tells that in various places a golden broodhen was worshipped. In some she sat on twelve golden eggs, elsewhere she had twelve golden chickens around her. The heathen priest held the golden brood-hen in great esteem. They kept guard over her day and night and listened whether she would make a sound. According to the mysterious noises that came from the golden hen's throat the priests constructed their prophesies. There was a golden hen in Levý Hradec too. So it was with fear that the heathen priests awaited Bořivoj's arrival. He was on

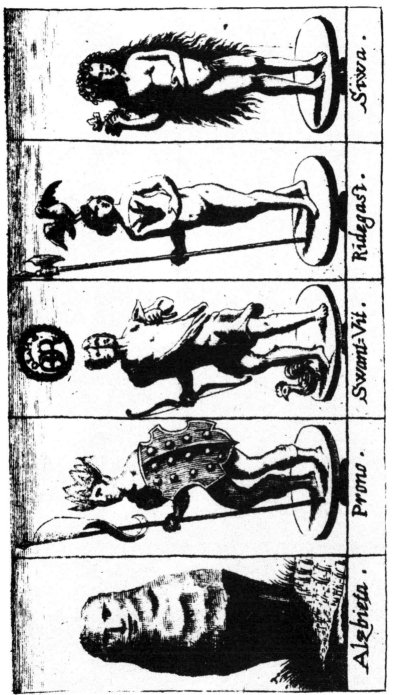

Pagan Idols

his way back from Moravia, from the mighty Svatopluk, and the story that preceded him said that he had been christened while with Svatopluk.

The day that messengers brought the news to Levý Hradec that Bořivoj's retinue was approaching the castle, the priests went out on the ramparts. A golden cross shone at the head of the princely procession. Terror seized the heathen priests. They ran in confusion from the castle before the Christian prince. But before they left they flung the golden brood-hen, together with her golden eggs, into a well, so that no one should find her. Then they filled in the well. And yet it is said that once in every hundred years the golden hen leaves the depths of the earth, runs across the grass over her hiding place and clucks three times. Then it disappears again for a hundred years. The heathen priests had to leave Tetín as well. Bořivoj ordered them out of the castle. The country was rid of heathen idols and priests, but the old faith still haunted the place and competed with the new.

One day Bořivoj was hunting in the Tetín woods and he and his huntsmen were following the tracks of a stag. The quiet forest was filled with the barking of dogs and the pounding of horses hoofs. The tracks led to a re-mote corner of the woods. Suddenly a doe burst out of the thicket instead of a stag. The dogs left the scent of the stag and rushed after the doe. The doe wound its way between the tree-trunks, ran to the river and into the water. The dogs stopped on the bank and Bořivoj and the huntsmen caught up with them. Bořivoj drew the string of his bow and unleashed an arrow. He wounded the doe in the flank and the dogs, as if they could scent their victim's blood from afar, leapt into the river and rushed after the wounded animal, with the huntsmen at their heels.

They struggled through the thickets on the other bank of the river up to a cliff overgrown with moss and lichen. And stood still in amazement. In front of a cave hollowed out of the cliff, almost overgrown with wild branches, stood a man. A long beard and long hair covered his face and his body was poorly clad. From the tangle of beard and hair his eyes glittered and the heavens were reflected in them as on the surface of a deep well. The wounded doe crouched at his lean bare feet. The man bent down to the doe, touched the painful place on her flank and the wound was healed.

The huntsmen were frightened at the strange apparition. They were visited by a memory of the heathen teaching and supposed that a spirit of the forest, a wild woodman, stood before them, a hobgoblin. But Bořivoj, who had been a Christian the longest of them, had seen such men of the Christian faith on his journeys to Svatopluk the Great. They were called hermits. They went into forests and lonely places so that no one should interrupt their religious meditations. Bořivoj recognised that he was facing a hermit, but memories of the heathen teaching smouldered in him too. So he asked :

"Who are you, a man or – ?"

"I am Ivan, a servant of God," replied the hermit.

"I have never seen you. Have you lived here long? And what do you live on in this deserted place?"

"I have been living here a long time," said the hermit, "but I do not seek out people and they do not seek for me. I live on what the forest affords me. Roots, berries and herbs. Heaven sent me this doe, so that I should gain strength from her milk. And you Sir, almost killed her."

Bořivoj understood that the man before him had renounced earthly joys to come nearer to his god through privation.

"Forgive me," he said to Ivan the hermit, "for wounding your doe. Come with me and you shall lack for nothing. I will give you bread and warm clothing, and you can live with me in my castle for as long as you wish."

"I need neither bread nor clothes," the hermit answered, "I have but one wish."

"I will fulfil anything in my power," promised Bořivoj.

"My wish is a modest one," said Ivan the hermit, "I wish that neither you nor your people should ever visit me again."

33

Bořivoj returned to Tetín in silence, deep in thought. The heathen belief, that he had rejected years ago, started to make itself felt again. He could not understand why the hermit sought God in misery and want. He told his wife about the strange meeting. And Ludmila asked about the hermit and was filled with admiration for his lonely, ascetic life. She determined that she would persuade the shy hermit to come to Tetín. She spared no effort and went secretly with a few servants to see Ivan the hermit, and she succeeded in persuading him to come to Tetín. He refused any escort, nor was anyone allowed to come and meet him. He set out for Tetín through woods and undergrowth, avoiding the paths, so as not to meet people. The arduous journey through pathless country, over hill and dale, tired the hermit. He came to Tetín late and had to stay overnight to rest. He received only Bořivoj and Ludmila in his castle chamber. And all night he told them about his faith.

At daybreak Ivan the hermit set out on his way back. Not far from the village of Hodyně he sat down on a stone beneath a wild pear-tree. And legend tells that the hard stone softened under him like a cushion, so that he should sit more comfortably.

Some herdsman drove a throng of horses to pasture by where he sat. As soon as they saw the hermit they began to laugh at him — at his bony figure, his beard, his long hair and threadbare clothes. The hermit rested quietly and took no notice of them. His defencelessness gave them courage. One of the herdsmen took up a stone and threw it at the hermit. It hit him on the temple. Blood started to flow down his cheek. Some drops of blood fell on the stone and stained it so that it could never be washed off.

Then the Hodyně farmer who owned the herd came to that place. When he saw what was going on, he punished the herdsmen and took care of the wounded man.

"Come to the village with me," he invited Ivan the hermit, "you can wash your wound, have some food and rest." He urged and insisted, but the hermit refused.

"If you wish to do me a service," Ivan said at last, to please the kind-hearted farmer, "lend me a horse, and I promise that I will return it before the day is out."

The farmer did not hesitate. He took a horse from the herd, saddled it and helped the hermit to mount. On horseback the hermit 's journey passed more quickly. When the horse had taken him up to the crest of the hill, he dismounted. From there he could see the tree-tops of the forest where his cave was. He stroked the horse and spoke to it:

"Run along, trot off home quickly!"

When he had been stroked and had heard those words, the horse began to grow, his shoulders and chest broadened, and when he started to trot he became a magnificent trotter, as if he had come from a royal stable.

The farmer's wife saw the horse running about the yard.

"Whose horse is that and where has it come from?" she wondered. The farmer recognised the horse by the saddle.

That day brought luck and prosperity to the farm that never left it.

Ivan the hermit visited Bořivoj and Ludmila several times more in Tetín castle. Otherwise he talked to no one and lived alone in his cave hidden in the woods. And that was where death found him. He was buried there and Prince Bořivoj had a church built over his grave.

Soon after that Bořivoj too went to join his ancestors. It is told that he died when he was thirty-six years old. And his was not the last death that Ludmila was to see.

After Prince Bořivoj his first-born son Spytihněv reigned. He became known for bringing a large number of western priests to the country, who served the mass in Latin. He established the church of St. Peter for them in the castle of Budeč. When he died prematurely, his younger brother Vratislav took the throne.

Prince Vratislav had St. George's church built in Prague castle. It became the custom to build churches and chapels in castles, and the power of the Christian

Et ego natus accepi Communem aerem, et in
similiter factam decidi terram, et primam
uocem Similem omnibus emisi plorans. *Sap.7. v.3.*

priests gradually ousted the power of the heathens.

And it was not only a time of churches, it was a time of death too. Prince Vratislav also died prematurely.

The strife between the old and the new continued.

The princely throne of Bohemia was empty. So Vratislav's wife, Princess Drahomíra, ascended the throne until Vratislav's sons should become of age. Their names were Wenceslas and Boleslav.

Wenceslas had been chosen to became prince of Bohemia even during Vratislav's lifetime. Boleslav was to be satisfied with the territory to the north of the river Elbe. But so far they were still boys.

Little Wenceslas was Ludmila's only joy. She preferred him to Boleslav, as he reminded her of her sons Spytihněv and Vratislav. She found gentleness and kindness in him, which were her own qualities. Boleslav was of a more violent nature, liking the bow and the sword much better than training his mind and reading books. Ludmila only understood Wenceslas. But Boleslav was understood by his mother, Drahomíra. She came of the tribe of the Elbe valley Stodorans, who had withstood the new Christian faith the longest and kept stubbornly to the heathen gods.

Whenever Ludmila went to her old paternal castle Pšov, she took little Wenceslas with her. There vineyards climbed up the slope facing the river. Some of the vines had been planted by Ludmila herself, she tended them and in the autumn plucked clusters of grapes from them. Little Wenceslas used to go to the vineyards with her, he helped her and learned how to look after the vines. Later, when he grew up, he and Ludmila made the wine that was needed for the ceremony of the Christian mass. And they planted new vineyards together.

The young Wenceslas learnt to read Slav lettering, but he could read Latin too. He learnt Latin at Budeč castle, from where Christian teaching spread, just as in old days heathen teaching had spread from there. Now priests from western countries taught the future Prince Wenceslas there. For long afterwards people would point out an oblong boulder on a stony slope not far from Budeč, on

Quem ab infantiâ timere Deum docuit,
et abstinere ab omni peccato. Tob. 1. ♦. 10.

which Wenceslas was said to have often rested when tired with learning.

After Vratislav's death much was changed. Wenceslas no longer met Ludmila in Prague castle, nor in Vyšehrad. She had left for Tetín for good, so as not to annoy the sight of Drahomíra, who showed her disfavour of her more and more. Drahomíra imagined many reasons why she hated Ludmila. She found Ludmila's gentleness hateful, considering it feminine weakness, she found Ludmila's fervour in matters of the Christian religion hateful, and she was afraid of her influence as a grandmother on her grandson Wenceslas.

Even now she was afraid of Wenceslas's gentleness and kindness. What sort of a prince will he be? she thought. Not a prince, but a monk, who will vacillate whenever he should grasp his sword and shed blood. And Drahomíra was jealous of Ludmila's grandson's love for her, and she was jealous too of the love the people had for Ludmila.

Legend tells that Christianity touched Princess Drahomíra only as a breeze touches the grass. Her spirit did not change with baptism. She was hard and unrelenting, taught by the constant battles of the tribe from which she came. She believed that whoever held the power held life, and she did not wish to share power with Ludmila. Neither power nor property.

So Ludmila's departure from Prague castle to Tetín castle was like flight. And that was when the time ripened for the whole of the Fate's prophesy to be fulfilled.

Drahomíra was not content with Ludmila's leaving. So long as Ludmila was alive her glory shone across the forests and the river even from Tetín castle. And with that glory lived everything that Drahomíra was afraid of and that aroused her hatred. She determined that she would quench Ludmila's glow with violence and would seize the entire heritage for herself.

She hired two murderers, who were named Tuna and Gomon. She commanded them to go to Tetín with a retinue, as if they had come on a friendly visit. Then, in the night, Tuna and Gomon were to betray the laws of

Ego autem totis uiribus meis præparaui im:
penſas domus DEI mei. 1. Paral.29. V. 2.

hospitality most terribly. Drahomíra promised them silver and estates after the deed was done.

Ludmila saw a group of horsemen ascending the hill to Tetín castle and a premonition of evil gripped her heart. She sought comfort in her faith for the suffering that was approaching her. For her weapons of faith were to replace the sword and dagger.

When the time came for dinner and the retinue with Tuna and Gomon sat down to table, Ludmila herself handed the food to her murderers and talked with them as if with friends. But they did not see her as a noble lady, who had once brought them up as her own sons and given them many gifts. In place of Ludmila they saw the silver and estates promised by Drahomíra.

At last evening fell on the Tetín forests and dusk entered the castle halls. Tuna and Gomon, hidden by darkness, set out to find Ludmila. Perhaps for the last time their consciences moved in them and put off the deed till the last moment, perhaps they hoped that darkness would not betray them as murderers, and would keep their faces and their names secret. And like all who wait for a long time, and take long to choose the right moment, they were suddenly overcome by impatience and were eager to finish what they had begun.

They learned that Ludmila had retired to her chamber to rest. They hurried there, broke down the door and rushed to her bedside. Terrified, Ludmila sat up in bed. She could not see who was approaching her in the dark, but she felt that it was death approaching. She turned to where she heard it, and begged:

"I ask only for a moment, so that I may pray."

And death waited a while.

Ludmila said her prayers and begged a second time:

"If I am to die, cut off my head with a sword."

She wished to shed her blood in the manner of martyrs.

But death did not fulfil her second request.

Tuna and Gomon tightened a noose round Ludmila's neck and strangled her with a rope they had brought with

Percuſſerunt me, et uulnerauerunt me, tulerüq;

pallium meum *Cant. 5. V. 7.*

them. Thus Ludmila died early on a Saturday night in the middle of the month of September.

The murderers, protected by Drahomíra's courtiers, leapt cheerfully onto their horses and galloped back that same night to Prague castle, to announce to the princess the news she was waiting for.

As soon as Drahomíra heard that the woman she hated was dead she rejoiced. She rewarded Tuna and Gomon with silver and gold, and gave them the estates they longed for. But she could not give them a mind at peace, comfort and happiness. In the midst of their splendour it was especially a peaceful mind that was lacking. The deed that each of them had equally on his conscience did not unite but divided them. A quarrel arose between them, and they quarrelled with Drahomíra too. Then Tuna fled the country from Gomon and wandered in foreign lands, where in the end he met a miserable death. Gomon later wanted to flee to save himself from Princess Drahomíra's anger, but his escape did not succeed. Drahomíra's servants caught him and he was executed. His offspring and relatives were killed and the silver, gold and estates passed into other hands. Property changes its owners, but a good reputation and honest name cannot change their owners.

The good reputation of the just and kindly Ludmila spread to all corners of our land and crossed its frontiers. It is told that a fragrance spread around her grave in Tetín, as if a thousand flowers blossomed in the atmosphere and as if it rained scented oil. And at night it would happen that the darkness was penetrated by a sudden glow, as of a flaring torch. Drahomíra heard of the strange happenings over Ludmila's grave and she was seized with anxiety. To drive away this anxiety she had a church built over the grave. And when Prince Wenceslas started to reign he sent a procession of priests and leading men of the people to lift Ludmila's relics and bring them to Prague castle. He had loved Ludmila during her life-time, and wished to have her near him after her death.

And what was the surprise of those who uncovered the grave! Legend tells that they found Ludmila's body there unharmed, as if she had just lain down to sleep. And it seemed to them that she would rise, come to life and speak. She did not come to life, she was smiling slightly, reconciled to her fate.

Her mouth fell silent. Her voice entered legend and fable, songs and books.

We too are forefathers of the human race
that will come after us, we too
are the forefathers of future forefathers and everything,
buildings and ruins, lies and truth
war and peace, cowardice and heroism,
will be found by those who come after us
in our half-buried tracks.
You may choose on which side of the scales
you will add your name.
We too, even today, are
the forefathers of forefathers.

THE TWO STARS

At the time when in our country the teaching about the one God was waging war with a great number of little heathen gods, Prince Wenceslas ascended the throne. It is told that his reign was a just one, he recognised one law for the rich and the poor, in quarrels he searched carefully and circumspectly for the guilty, inclined always to the side of mercy. He never ordered that prisoners be tortured, for he had sympathy with every human pain and every sorrow. At a time when so many princes invented cruel punishments and avenged themselves through punishment, Prince Wenceslas forgave and invented help instead of punishment.

46

❋ *Eo tempore terebat in area triticum.* ɟ. paral. 21. V. 20.

Collegit ergo in agro usq̃ ad uesperam: et quæ collegerat uirga cædẽs
et excutiens, inuenit quasi ephi mensurã, id est tres modios. Ruth. 2. V. 17. et 18.

His deeds reflected Ludmila's gentle nature, just as the indomitable character of Princess Drahomíra lived on in Boleslav's deeds. While Boleslav spurred his horse after deer in the leafy woods on the banks of the Elbe, Wenceslas ground wheat in a handmill, kneaded dough from the flour and made wafers for the Christian mass. It sometimes happened at great festivals, when mass christenings were held, that only few children came to be baptized. Then the prince sent his servants to the Prague slave-market, telling them to buy all the children out of slavery and christen them. It was an ancient custom to hunt game in the forest, but it was not a custom to buy child slaves, nor was it a custom to show mercy to culprits or to call on the Christian God. That is why those who loved the old ways grumbled about Prince Wenceslas and took his gentleness for weakness. They did not understand that even a coward may shout: To battle, to battle! and that a dauntless man follows his star silently and steadfastly.

When the disagreements between Wenceslas's adherents and opponents threatened to overflow their banks like a spring flood, the prince intervened, though unwillingly and sorrowfully. He commanded his mother, Drahomíra, to depart for Budeč castle. Wenceslas's advisers saw Drahomíra as the main obstacle to reconciliation. And indeed, with their support gone, the party of Wenceslas's opponents calmed down. But it was only a surface calm, the enemies had learnt how to pretend a truce. But in the very neighbourhood of the Bohemian princedom, on the territory of the Zlicko prince, there was a growing desire to conquer a bit of Bohemian soil from Prince Wenceslas. The Zlicko prince, named Radslav whose seat was Kouřim castle, led his army out against the Bohemians and started to besiege Bohemian fortresses. He supposed that the peaceful Prince Wenceslas would retreat and the men of Zlicko would gain an easy victory.

News was brought to Prague castle of the Zlicko army's advance. Prince Wenceslas's heart was heavy. He did not love bloodshed, but he could not allow wrong-doing. So

Samuel autem miniſtrabat ante faciem
Domini Puer accinctus ephod lineo .1.Reg .2. .V.18.

he called for the people to be assembled and he placed himself at the head of the Bohemian army and went to war against Radslav of Kouřim. On the road both young and old joined Wenceslas's army with weapons in their hands and called for the blood of the enemy. These bloodthirsty words reached Wenceslas, who rode his horse with bowed head. In that call for revenge he heard the cawing of the rooks and carrion-crows that fly around the battlefield after a fight. He heard the calls for plunder that has not the value of a human life. And he saw, striding amongst his warriors, those who were to fall. Before his eyes the swords of the Zlicko men were measured against the swords of the Bohemians, were plunged into chests and the blood of the enemy was mixed with the blood of friends. Prince Wenceslas felt grief, for his heart counted the dead on both sides and did not distinguish the Bohemians from the men of Zlicko in death.

And so the prince with the Bohemian army came to the place where they saw in the distance the approaching crowds of the Zlicko men stirring up the dust on the parched ground. As he looked at the armed men, closing in from both sides like two clouds, Wenceslas lit on a good idea. He designated messengers quickly and sent them to Radslav with a strange message.

"Tell him," Prince Wenceslas told the messengers, "that there is no need for so many deaths for one of us to be victorious in battle. Let him save his own and my people, and if he yearns for weapons to decide, let him ride out to meet me alone. Let the princes fight and the armies wait. If Radslav wins, let him rule my princedom, if I win he will hand over his princedom to me."

The messengers told Radslav without delay what Wenceslas asked of them, Radslav listened to the messengers and was amazed. Never had he heard that the victory or defast of two armies should be decided by a duel of princes. But he could not refuse Wenceslas's request. If he refused he would prove himself a coward. So he commanded the advance of the Zlicko throng to stop, and promised Wenceslas's messengers that he would come to

NON MORTE SED ARTE

*Apparuerunt aduersarijs de cœlo uiri, ex quibus duo Ma-
chabæum medium habentes, armis suis circum septum
incolumem conseruabant. 2. Machab. 10. V. 29. et 30.*

the destined place. Let prince fight with prince and their struggle decide the victor.

And both armies stood still and the space between them was flooded with the sun of truce. War entered the two princes. They rode out from the heart of their columns and the warriors, leaning in their shields and lances, watched the dancing steps of the princes' horses. Then the horses broke into a trot and it seemed that the princes would come into collision and the raised swords would find their goal. But suddenly Radslav reined in his horse so sharply that its hoofs dug into the dusty soil. He lowered his sword and leapt to the ground. He leapt to the ground, laid his naked sword on the grass and knelt as a sign that he humbled himself before Wenceslas. And Wenceslas jumped from his horse too, raised Radslav from the ground and said: "If you long for reconciliation as I long for it, retreat with your people and be satisfied with what belongs to you, leave alone what is not yours."

Radslav returned to his own men and commanded them to return to Zlicko territory. The Zlicko band retreated, but their leaders complained of Prince Radslav.

"Why did he not use his sword against the Bohemian prince?" they scolded. "Why did he get down from his horse and kneel, as if he were afraid of Wenceslas? He surrendered without a fight," they fulminated, "and did not try to get in even a single blow."

Radslav heard what they were saying and answered:

"How could I raise my sword? My hand dropped of itself. Suddenly the sword was as heavy as heaven and earth together. My hand fell and I saw a golden cross on Prince Wenceslas's forehead and on either side of him there floated two splendid winged figures. Then I understood that Prince Wenceslas is a just man, and the just are under the protection of heaven."

Nor was there any lack of irate voices in Wenceslas's army. Those who had come out to do battle longed for booty, and they could not forgive Prince Wenceslas that he had not made use of Radslav's humiliation.

Hymnus de S. Wenceslao.

Swatý Wáclawe/ Weywodo Cze-
Sancte Wenceslae, Princeps Terræ

ské Země/ Knižená§: pro§ za ná§ Boha/
Boëmæ, Dux noster: Deum e xo ra,

Swa té ho Ducha/ Kyrie e leyſon.
Sacrofanctů Pnevma, Kyrie eleiſon.

But Prince Wenceslas's longings took other paths. He founded Christian churches and began to build the church of St. Vitus in Prague castle. It is told that the prince dreamt of a life of retirement in some Roman monastery. This monkish dream, his care for churches, the peace he concluded with the German king, his will to maintain peace and calm, all that angered Wenceslas's enemies. The heroism that despises everything but itself is nearer to people's hearts than prudence, that is the true mother of heroes.

While Wenceslas watched the walls of the St. Vitus' church grow in Prague castle, his younger brother lived in a castle on the northern bank of the river Elbe. That castle had once been founded by Vratislav on an extremely advantageous site, for it was naturally sheltered on three sides. From the south, west and north it was protected by deep tarns, treacherous swamps and a branch of the Elbe. Only on the eastern side was the castle protected by a rampart, the work of human hands. Vratislav had left the castle and the land around it to his son Boleslav. It was forested land, rich in game and crying out to be hunted. It was land neighbouring on the old Pšov territory on the western side and the territory of the Croats on the east. It was land on the very edge of the Bohemian princedom, and Boleslav's castle guarded the Elbe ford on the road to Prague.

Large, thick and dark were the forests around the Elbe and the Jizera rivers, but greater and darker was Boleslav's ambition. He was among those who did not wish Wenceslas the rule of the country. Those who were dissatisfied would visit the castle on the Elbe and Boleslav would always listen to them. And he was himself incessantly dissatisfied with his position and with the place that Vratislav had given him while he was still alive.

One day he summoned the leaders of his people to his castle, and when they were assembled he mounted a raised place and spoke:

"I have had you summoned to make my will known to you. Look around you, you see wooden fortifications, a

Conterebam molas iniqui, et de dentibus illi-
us auferebam prædam. Job 29. v. 17.

wooden castle."

The older people looked around them and failed to understand Boleslav's words. The castle was wooden, but that was how Boleslav's father Vratislav had had it built. It was not then the custom to build in any other way than from what the nearby forest provided.

"We do not understand you, Sire," said the elders.

"I have seen that elsewhere they build fortifications of stone, after the Roman manner. And that is what you will build for me — stone bulwarks, a stone castle."

"We shall build as our fathers built," said the elders, "and may the gods grant us that our sons too will build that way."

These words enraged Boleslav, anger bade him draw his sword and run amongst the assembled elders. Their eyes were determined and relentless, they observed Boleslav in silence. Cruel anger bid Boleslav a second time. He grasped the nearest elder by the hair and with one sweep of his sword he separated the old man's head from his body. He lifted the head he had chopped off and showed it to the crowd.

"This head refused obedience to me," he cried, "but my sword will never cease to obey me!"

The elders, frightened by Boleslav's deed, fell to their knees and loudly promised obedience. That same day they told their people of Boleslav's wish and started to make preparations for building. And it is told that Boleslav built a castle to which he gave his name, and he ordered that a chapel of SS. Cosma and Damian should be built within the castle. When the day came of those saints to whose honour the chapel had been dedicated, Boleslav took the opportunity and invited Prince Wenceslas to his castle. He knew that his godly elder brother would not refuse.

On the last September Sunday Prince Wenceslas mounted his horse and set off with his retinue from Prague castle to Boleslav castle. They crossed the river Vltava, forded the Rokytnice stream and entered the forest that stretched as far as the Elbe.

Si despexi praetereuntem, eo quod non habuerit indu-
mentum, et absque operimento pauperem, si non be-
nedixerunt mihi latera eius. Job. 31. V. 19. et 20.

The sun was caught in the treetops and revealed the first yellowing leaves and every moment the prince and his company had to wipe delicate cobwebs from their faces. On all sides the glory of autumn was beginning to flame and that glory meant destruction. The prince's company anxiously observed the signs of approaching winter and argued as to whether a frosty or a kindly winter awaited them. The prince was silent. An invisible companion sat with him in his saddle and its name was: care.

The last water they had to cross was the Elbe. And here, as if the sight of the river that announced the end of their journey had shaken an unknown weight from the prince's shoulders, he spurred on his horse so that they should enter his brother's castle gate as soon as might be.

Hardly had the hoofs of Wenceslas's horse touched the opposite bank and Boleslav's castle could be seen between the branches, than an unknown man leapt out of the thicket, stood in the prince's path and called:

"Sire, a fresh horse is waiting in the bushes. I beseech you, take it and ride as quickly as you may back to Prague. Boleslav will let you into his castle alive, but you will not leave it alive. Hurry, go back, save yourself!"

"I know not who you are," replied the prince, "but I believe you. I know my younger brother has no love for me. But, my unknown friend, how could I want something other than God wants, who guides my fate?"

And Prince Wenceslas waved to the unknown man and rode on to the castle.

That day the castle had two faces. One apparent, festive, hospitable and friendly, the other cunningly hidden, lying in wait for the right moment, treacherous. Boleslav too had two faces. He received Wenceslas in friendship and took him into the hall, where everything was ready for a feast. They ate and drank and wine soon washed away the caution of the enemies. Hidden swords now and then showed their blades, glittered and disappeared again in the folds of a cloak. Three times did Boleslav's conspirators rise, determined to attack Prince Wenceslas, and three times they sank back into their seats.

Die noctuq; æstu urebar et gelu, fugiebatq; sommus
ab oculis meis. Gen. 31. V. 40.
Qui dat niuem sicut lanam. psal. 147. V. 16.

It was already dusk when the prince left the banqueting hall to refresh himself with fresh air. The unknown man again approached him out of the shadows and whispered:

"Sire, there is still time, you still have an opportunity, perhaps the last. Hasten, get on your horse and we will ride away together in the darkness."

But instead of an answer the prince went back to the banqueting hall, proposed a toast, kissed all those at the table, both friends and foes, and went to his bed.

Wenceslas and his company slept, Boleslav met with his men for consultation. The night covered their arguments with a black wing. At last an early morning hour was decided on, when the prince would go to the church for morning prayers. And they called on the priest of that church to lock the church door.

At dawn , before the sky had rubbed the mist from its eyes, Prince Wenceslas rose from his bed, dressed himself quickly and hurried to the church for his morning devotions. On the way he met his brother Boleslav.

"God give you health, brother!" he called with a smile and began to thank Boleslav for yesterday's feast.

But Boleslav was prepared to feast his brother on iron. He drew his sword and struck. But it so happened that he wounded the prince only slightly. Wenceslas gripped his brother's arm, twisted the sword from his fingers and forced him to his knees.

"I do not want to pay you back in kind," said the prince, "put away your anger and let us part in peace." At these words he handed his brother the sword he had just taken from him and continued on his way to the church.

Boleslav, upset by what had happened, could not find the strength to repeat the attack. So he started shouting, to call his friends who were waiting in ambush. They rushed from their hiding-place and their hungry swords reached Wenceslas in front of the church door. As a last hope the prince grasped the ring of the door handle, to open it and find shelter in the church. The door was locked. Gripping the handle, he received the blows

Consurrexit Cain aduersus Fratrem suum Abel,
et interfecit eum. Gen. 4. V. 8.

without defending himself. Not even when he breathed his last did he fall in the dust before his murderers. His hand never left the ring on the church door. The handle of a church door had all his life been nearer to him than the hilt of a sword.

There his attackers left him and fled. The noise awoke the priest Kastěje. He did not know what was happening. He went out into the castle courtyard, now empty and quiet, and saw blood by the church door and the prince's body, motionless, lifeless. Horrified, he sought out Wenceslas's mother, Drahomíra, and together they took the dead man to her quarters. They washed the body and laid it in the church with tears.

By then Boleslav's castle had woken up and disturbance reigned everywhere. Boleslav's company mercilessly persecuted those who had come with Prince Wenceslas, and killed them on the threshold of the new day. On that Monday, 28th September 935, there was as much blood spilt as in a battle with an enemy. And when Boleslav's supporters had settled with Wenceslas's friends, they rode to Prague and continued their bloody work even there. Drahomíra, warned in time, fled from Boleslav's castle to the tribe of the Croats. She could not be sure of her life. Boleslav had Wenceslas's body hastily buried and hurried to Prague to become the prince himself.

Legend relates that that same day they carefully washed all traces of blood from the walls of the church and the ground. But in a short while blood again appeared in the same places. They washed it away again, and again it appeared like a red sun out of autumn mists. It is said to have appeared for a long time in memory of that evil deed. And it is related too that Wenceslas's most faithful servant, Podiven, fled from his persecutors to Germany. He spent a long time there in mourning, but when he thought that calm had returned to the Bohemian princedom he returned home. Then he walked along paths that he had trod with Prince Wenceslas. And the more he remembered his prince the less he found himself able to forgive his murderers.

Quodcunq, invenerit manus tua, da servis tuis. 1.Reg.25.V.8.

Extendit manum suam in retribuendo. psal.54.V.21.

Here it was, he said dejectedly to himself, this is where we wandered in snow and frost. When I complained that my feet were freezing, the prince advised me to place my feet in his footsteps. I did as he suggested and I felt as though I were walking through a summer-warmed meadow. Podiven remembered and hatred grew in his heart like a mighty plant. He grabbed his sword and ran to the house where one of Wenceslas's murderers lived. He found him in a steam bath and pierced him through on the spot. Then he fled to the dense forest.

When Boleslav heard that one of his friends had been killed by Podiven, he had the forest where Podiven was hiding surrounded. In the thickets they chased Wenceslas's servant Podiven like a wild animal. And at the place where they found him they straight-way hanged him.

It was then said amongst the people that Podiven hung on a tree for three years and not even a bird touched him, nor a beast of prey, nor putrefaction. They said that his beard and nails grew and his hair gradually receded and turned white. At last Boleslav had Podiven's body buried, but he could not bury his fame.

Wenceslas's murderers too lived on in people's mouths. All of them suffered an unlucky fate. Legend relates that one of them, of the name of Hněvsa, built an estate not far from the Elbe. He did not manage it in peace. Madness assailed him several times a year and his descendants all had red hair, in memory of the blood spilt. Another murderer, whose name is said to have been Štyrsa, fell into the earth together with his horse, his dog and his hawk, in the woods near Stará Boleslav. Nothing remained of him but the hole, which closed over and was soon covered with grass. ·And it was said that whoever went that way on the anniversary of the day of Prince Wenceslas's death heard strange noises. From the depths of the earth came the neighing of a horse, the barking of a dog and the tinkle of a hawk's bell. Other conspirators are said to have gone deaf or shrivelled alive, and others left this world in anguish.

After a time Prince Boleslav decided that his dead brother's body should be brought to Prague and laid in the church of St. Vitus. He told his servants to take Wenceslas from Boleslav castle at night, secretly. And it is told that the cart drove out with the dead prince furtively at dead of night from the castle gates with an armed escort, as if they were taking precious loot that may not be touched by a ray of sun. The cart came to the Elbe, and that night the level of the water rose and it flooded over the meadows. It was not within human power to reach the other side through the rushing, foaming torrent. But suddenly the river was not in front of the cart, but behind it. The waggoners were amazed. Their feet were dry, and dry too were the wheels of the cart, despite the river's being behind them. They hurried on their way till they reached the stream called Rokytnice. The Rokytnice too had flooded its banks and wild waves heaved and surged where the ford was. Boleslav's servants stood helpless on the bank. And as had happened the first time, so it happened again. The cart suddenly stood with its waggoners on the opposite bank and could continue on its way.

And when dawn came they saw that the river Vltava lay behind them, and they were unable to explain it. So the cart with the dead prince passed over three storm-tossed rivers that the prince had crossed in his lifetime one sunny September Sunday. And the legends tell of many miracles. The sick and the crippled who had formerly made pilgrimages to Wenceslas's grave in Boleslav now made pilgrimages to Prague, to the church of St. Vitus. But then the famous vast cathedral of St. Vitus was not yet standing, and the pilgrims soon filled the crowded area of the church and the space before it. Pilgrims even came from abroad. There is a story told of a man from the land of France, who had dragged himself along on crutches for years and in Prague he found his long-lost health at the grave of Prince Wenceslas. There were many tales and reports of miracles and far and wide people began to speak of the dead prince as a saint.

Prince Boleslav was alive and well. His path was not

S.Václav.

steeped in the scent of incense and the singing of psalms. He had other cares. He was waiting for an opportunity to fight a battle that would bring him victory. And his time came.

Two columns of the army of the young German King Otto were advancing on Bohemia. Boleslav defeated them like a brave commander. For twice seven years he tore Bohemia from its union with the German empire and extended his own power to large territories beyond the borders of Bohemia.

And it is told how, after twice seven years, Otto I. again led his army into Bohemia and besieged Boleslav's castle on the Elbe. The castle was solid for its time and well protected by water and banked-up earthworks and a rampart and it was not easy to conquer it. A July sun scorched the landscape and the heat troubled the besieged and the besiegers. The castle garrison was commanded by Prince Boleslav's son, who was named after his father. He was to take over the rule from his father too. Day by day the supplies in the castle grew less, and in the evenings clouds of mosquitoes rose from the drying swamps in the meadows. The time was coming when the besieged garrison expected a decisive attack. But the king did not attack. He waited. His spies brought news that Prince Boleslav was bringing troops to help his son. The king waited. It was more favourable for his to await the prince's arrival and start negotiations with him than to try and conquer the castle. Legend tells that the king and the prince agreed on a truce and together they entered Boleslav's castle to seal the renewed union between the Bohemian prince and the German empire. It is said that a throne was erected for King Otto I. in the castle courtyard, at the place where a stone lion stands today. Prince Boleslav bound himself to pay moneys to Germany, as Prince Wenceslas had done. In this way he rid his country of the constant threat from the west. At least for some time. But that time was decisive for the unification of the country under one prince and for the emergence of the Bohemian state.

Žiwot a Sláwa
Swatého
Wácslawa
Mučedlnjka/ Knjžete/ Krale/ a Pátrona Cžeského.

Wydaný

W Latinské Ržečj/od Ctihodného Knéze/Jana Tannera z Towaryšstwa Gežjssowa.

A nynj

Pro potéssenj Duchowni/wsseho Cžeského Národu/ gessto Latinské Ržečj newmégj/ a pro wzbuzenj wétssj pobožnostl k Swatému Wácslawu/ yákožto Dědičnému Patronu.

W Cžesstinu vwedený

Od Knéze Felixa Kadlinského/z téhož Towaryšstwa Gežjssowa.

Wytisstěný w Praze/ w Impressy Universitatis, w Kollegi Towaryšstwa Gežjssoweho/bliž Mostu/ Léta 1702.

Mercilessly advancing time gave the two princely brothers new names. Boleslav, who had had his brother murdered at his castle, began to be called "the Cruel" and Prince Wenceslas, whom the church had declared a saint, began to be called "the Holy". Since that time two stars have shone over Bohemia and Moravia, each with a different light. The first made trumpets sound and drums and pennants fly, and the second illuminated the foreheads of thinkers and the soft sibilance of quills with which the scribe drew his letters. And the time that would link the glimmer of the two stars was yet to come.

IHS

O Dědicý České Země
Rozpomen se na swé Ble me,

Pod swau Ochranu se vtícam

Swaty WACLAWE
Weywodo České Země: Knjže náš, pros za
nás Boha!

S. Adalberd.

The Life

of St. Adalbert

BEATVS ADALBERVS VIRGO CONFES: 3 MARTYR

Wherever you go you carry within yourself
the country you came from,
wherever you go you bear that country,
the land you dream of and long for.
That was the first and still is,
the second is yet to be
and nowhere in the world can you find it,
that future land, dreamland, happy land.
The kernel of the nut is everywhere hidden in its shell,
but at home the shells are hardest,
only at home do the sweetest kernels ripen.

THE DISTANT HOMELAND

The sword of Prince Boleslav I. did not tire. He left his son, Boleslav II., a vast Czech empire. It included Bohemia, Moravia, Slovakia and the Cracow region. Boleslav II. accepted his heritage, but the sword that fell from his dying father's languid fingers he took reluctantly, with hesitation. Boleslav II. supported the Christian religion, he founded the Prague bishopric and time assigned him the name "the Pious". In those times a mighty castle stood at the confluence of two rivers, the Elbe and the Cidlina. It was named Libice. In that castle lived an offspring of the ancient family of Zlicko princes, Slavník. His estates were far-reaching, and were protected by frontier castles.

On the Bohemian border a castle stood on the hill Osek, against the Germans were the border castles Chýnov, Dúdleby and Netolice, on the Moravian border Litomyšl and against Poland Kladsko castle.

Libice castle was the seat of the lord of that region, Slavník, and his wife Střezislava and the members of their family. They were called after them the Slavníks. The Slavníks lived in friendship with the Prague prince and voluntarily recognized his sovereignty. But the wealth and power of the Slavníks hid danger within them. As a magnate Slavník maintained contact with the Polish and the German empires and messengers came to Libice from foreign lands and important visitors. Great feasts were held at Libice and the renown of the splendour of Slavník's court crossed the frontiers of Bohemia. Slavník enjoyed plenty in everything, but above his riches in lands and fortune he excelled in richness of mind. And he bequeathed this richness of mind to his sons, as others bequeath a sword. And there were seven of those sons, like the days of the week, and the most worthy of admiration was the one who had the name Adalbert.

In tender youth Adalbert had fallen prey to an evil sickness. Fever coursed through him and burnt all his youthful strength. He lay motionless on his bed and his breath rose and fell irregularly like the wing of a bird that has been shot.

Adalbert's parents stood by his bed and they heard death shuffling impatiently in the corner of the room. In the greatest of anxiety they fell to their knees at the bedside, they called on God and promised him they would dedicate their son to him if he would save him. And then it happened that Adalbert recovered, and his parents led him along the path of their promise.

In Libice Adalbert was taught by his tutor Radla. But before long the pupil knew as much as his teacher, and the teacher had no more to teach him. In those days there was a famous school in Magdeburg. And there his parents sent the young Adalbert, far into the German land, to be educated in the sciences of the

Quasi rosa plantata iuxta riuos aquarum.
Ecclesiastici cap: 39. V. 17.

time and the Christian religion. Knowledge and religion were so closely linked then, that the first led to the second and there was no knowledge without religion.

Adalbert left Libice, his region and the Bohemian land for the first time. He was young and full of expectation and hope. He as yet had no idea that it was to become his destiny to leave the country where he was born.

Adalbert lived in Magdeburg for many years and the boy became a young man. All that linked him to his old country were memories and the river Elbe. Its silver surface glinted beneath his native Libice castle, just as it did in Magdeburg, where the river flowed on its passage to the sea. But memories of his native land were gilded by distance, and the water in the river had long been different and foreign.

After nine years, Adalbert returned to his homeland. His father was no longer alive. He found only his mother and his brothers. Joy and grief accompanied him to the familiar places. The old castle now seemed small to Adalbert after the years he had spent abroad. Everything was different from what he had imagined at a distance. Even the people. They had been baptized and went to church for mass, but inside, in their hearts and heads, they were pagans as before. Now Adalbert realized that the country he had dreamed of in the German land was the distant country of his dreams. And he longed to change his dreams into reality.

He left for Prague and there received holy orders. Even in Prague he fared no better. There was talk that he was too strict. They did not approve of his uncompromising character. He condemned slavery, so the slave traders hated him. He condemned the dissolute life of the priests, and thus alienated many priests. He preached against paganism, and secret pagans saw him as an enemy. But he had friends too, who wished him well and respected what others hated.

When Bishop Dětmar of Prague died, Boleslav II. summoned an assembly of lords, temporal and spiritual. He

Pro puero isto oraui & dedit mihi Domin, pe
titionem meam. 1. Reg: 1. v. 27.

Car: Screta delin.   I. Caspa. Doons sculpsit

summoned them to Levý Hradec, where the first church founded in Bohemia stood.

From every direction representatives of the clans, nobles and priests gathered and Levý Hradec came to life as in the days of its princely glory. They gathered to consult on whom they should propose as bishop of Prague. The consultation was a short one. All of them called for Adalbert to become bishop.

Adalbert resisted such an honor. He was shy and did not love worldly fame, that foam which prevents the eyes from penetrating the depths of people and the world.

But there was then no more learned, distinguished and more worthy successor to Dětmar's throne. He could not refuse his election and accepted. In his twenty-fifth year he became a bishop.

When he returned from Italy, where he had been consecrated, he was welcomed home in the streets of Prague with cheering and song. This time, Adalbert's native land showed him her sweet side. Adalbert received it modestly. The young bishop, barefoot and silent, lost in his own thoughts and resolutions, made his way as the centre of the roaring crowd's attention. He yearned for perfection not only for himself, but for all those who waved to him. But this was a task beyond the strength of one man.

And there are reports of the young bishop's abstemiousness, his self-denying life and his care for the poor. But his efforts and longings met which misunderstanding and his preaching found only ears and not hearts. Thus his country showed him her bitter side.

After the death of his mother Střezislava, Adalbert left Bohemia again. He left a country where he had failed in eradicating the slave trade, pagan customs and laws. He left for Rome and there he and his brother Radim entered a monastery. Even though he would return to Bohemia two years later, leaving his country was to become his fate.

In Hungary, he baptized the local prince and his family. Once when he was in the Hungarian countryside, he looked down from a hill on a crowd of Hungarian pagans who were bowing down to worship a huge idol hewn out

PECPS

Puer autem crescebat, & confortabatur
plen, sapientiâ; & gratia Dei erat in illo
Lucæ Cap. 2. v. 40.

of a tree-trunk. He descended the hill, great and vener-
able as he was, pushed his way through the throng and
made straight for the wooden idol. A fire was flaming in
front of the idol. Adalbert picked up a burning branch
and set the statue on fire. The flame flared up from the
idol, and the crowd, dumbfounded with terror, dared not
even move.

Adalbert was dauntless in his struggle against old customs, but he was saddened on his frequent travels abroad
and saddened on his returns to his native land, where
conditions were not changing in the way he wished. Adalbert's life was like a wave that runs to the longed-for
shore, and the shore sends it back because it made too
great haste.

Once when Adalbert was again absent from his native
land, disaster struck his clan and his family castle Libice.
And this disaster was like a storm for which clouds gather
for a long time and at the most incredible moment, light-
ning strikes.

In the Litoměřice region lived the noble Vršovec clan,
which had great power at Boleslav's court. The Vršovec
clan was envious of the Slavník clan's estates, wealth, and
position in Bohemia. They knew that Boleslav II. would be
pleased to rule the Slavník land, just as he ruled his own
castles and lands. But no opportunity offered for them to
carry out the deed they had long yearned for.

In the last decade of the tenth century the German
ruler was preparing a campaign against the pagans. Two
military corps from Bohemia set out to help him. One
was commanded by the son of Boleslav II., and the other
by Slavník's oldest son, Soběbor. At Slavník's castles only
the most essential garrisons remained. No one suspected
anything untoward and the sky was blue that autumn and
augured calm.

On a pleasant sunny September day a lone horseman
galloped up to Libice castle. He brought bad news. Not
far from the castle the Prague prince's army, led by the
Vršovec clan, was marching through the woods. No one at
Libice could believe it. The forest stood motionless in the

Si putavi aurum robur meum, et obrizo dixi:
fiducia mea. Job. c: 31. ℣ 24.

sun, and the two shining arms of the river seemed to have ceased their flow and silently reflected the calm of the shining sky. It seemed as though a protective hand of the deepest peace was held over the castle and the countryside. Then the sound of a horn resounded from the castle tower. The guard was sounding the alarm. From the forest armed horsemen began to ride out onto the spreading meadows below the castle, behind them ran foot soldiers with spears and shields, and impatient archers could be seen raising their bows against Libice, testing their bowstrings and seeking targets.

Whoever at Libice had a strong arm seized his weapon and ran to the ramparts to defend his castle. More and more armed men came from the forest, and they were superior in numbers. They surrounded the castle and hurled themselves into battle. Legend tells that at that moment Boleslav II. lay on his bed in Prague struck down by apoplexy, only half understanding what was happening in his country. The monk who wiped the sweat from his brow and the spittle from this mouth could well have ruled in his stead, if he had so wished. So power lay in the hands of the Vršovec clan.

The following day was the feast of St. Wenceslas, and the besieged men begged for a truce. But the besiegers replied:

"Our lord is not Wenceslas, but Boleslav."

And they threw themselves against the ramparts like wolves scenting rich spoils. The defenders stood up to them bravely, fighting over every bit of the fortifications, then over every part of the courtyard, every bit of wall, every log hut. Finally the last defenders, Adalbert's four brothers, Spytimír, Pobraslav, Porej and Čáslav, took the advice of their old tutor Radla and fled into the church. It was the custom that anyone who sought refuge in a church might not be harmed by his pursuers.

The Vršovec men pounded on the church door and called:

"Come out and we will spare you. Who will give you food on the altar steps, who will give you drink? The

A. Castrum Lyphez. B. Arcus aquidum. C. Porta quæ gram. Lyphæ appellata. D. Balneum Lyphing. E. Lybicrum spiritus. f. Ecclesia B. Mariæ Virg. G. Domus ru olim. H. Ecclesia S. Georgii. I. Stipes vinea. K. Strata. L. Loca Lyphingi. M. Villa Alba. convenu O. ortum nieruum cum serpente A. flumini min Albi.

castle is in our hands. Come out and we will show you mercy. Nothing will happen to you."

Spytimír, Pobraslav, Porej and Čáslav believed this promise and came out of the church. Immediately armed men leapt on them and treacherously slaughtered them.

The Slavník clan had been butchered and Prince Boleslav II. now ruled their territory too. From his newly acquired estates he awarded the Vršovec clan for their merit in the fall of the Slavníks. Libice castle too was given them. But the misery and ruin they had cast upon the Slavníks rained down on their own heads after some years. Vršovec blood was spilt in Libice, they too were massacred within those same walls. Only three brothers of the Slavník family survived, being abroad at the time. These were the commander Soběbor, Radim and bishop Adalbert.

When, after a lapse of time, the Polish ruler Boleslav the Bold seized power in the Czech Lands, the Slavník Soběbor came back to Bohemia with the Polish army. After years in exile he stood in Prague castle and hoped his fate would turn. But the Polish army did not remain long in Bohemia. The German emperor had other intentions for the Czech Lands. He advanced on Prague with his army and with two members of the Přemyslide family, Jaromír and Oldřich. The Poles had to leave Prague castle in haste. It took Soběbor longer to take leave of his native land. He did so with sword in hand. He stood on the bridge across the castle moat and covered the retreat of his Polish companions. Here he fell with his weapon in his hand, just as his brothers had once fallen at Libice.

His brother Adalbert never again returned to Bohemia. He had no wish to return to the country that had become the grave of his clan, to a country where violence, murder, and treachery maintained the power of one clan over another. His homeland lived on in his great vision of a just society of noble-minded people. People who do not sacrifice their neighbours, but are willing to sacrifice themselves.

Egredere de terra tua, et de cognatione tua, et de domo pa-
tris tui: et ueni in terram quam monstrabo tibi. Gen: 12. V: 1.

He went to Poland, and from there to the pagan Prussians, to fulfil his dream with deeds. Dauntlessly he entered pagan territory and stepped without fear into a field concentrated to the pagan gods. As he did so shrieks were heard, and the pagans, who had followed Adalbert, fell on him with axes and spears. Under the blows of their weapons Adalbert gave up his soul.

The Polish ruler bought bishop Adalbert's body for gold, and had him buried in the town of Gniezno. The fame of Adalbert's name increased still further after his death, and his final resting-place also became famous. It is said that the German emperor, seeing Gniezno castle from a distance, and the church where Adalbert's relics were laid, jumped down from his horse and walked to the church barefoot.

Adalbert, son of the Slavníks of Libice castle, the learned Bohemian bishop, was declared a saint.

The youngest of the Slavníks, Radim, is said later to have become archbishop of Gniezno cathedral. And when he died the last light of the Slavník clan was extinguished. And yet once such a bright glow of mind and might had come from Libice, that the Slavník castle was in every way the equal of the castle of the Prague prince.

Sicut aqua effusus sum: et dispersi sunt omnia ossa mea.
Psalm . 21 . V . 15 .

Ossa ipsius Visitata sunt et post mortem
Prophetaverunt. Eccli c: 49 V: 18

Hæc requies mea in sæculum sæculi : hic habitabo, quoniam elegi eam . Psal. 131 . V. 14 -

EDUARD PETIŠKA:
A TREASURY OF TALES FROM THE KINGDOM OF BOHEMIA

Would you like to learn of the ancient history
of the famous Bohemian kingdom?
To enter the enchanting world of ancient legends?
To read of great Bohemian kings, saints, knights
and the ordinary people of the Czech Lands?

A Treasury of Tales from the Kingdom of Bohemia is the name
of the book that invites you on a journey into the world of Czech
legends. Here a great story-teller brings you exciting stories of
bygone centuries, describes events in the ancient mighty kingdom
of Bohemia. The captivating stories contained in this book have
originated over long centuries, since mythical times. Rare draw-
ings, not published in centuries, add to the charm
of this remarkable book.

The stories may also be used
as an excellent tourist guide for visitors to Bohemia.

Orders for the Czech, English and German versions
can be sent to the distributors
Baset
U Sanopzu 5
15000 Prague 5
The Czech Republic

The Baset network also distributes three unique books of
Prague stories:

EDUARD PETIŠKA, JAN M. DOLAN:
BEAUTIFUL STORIES OF GOLDEN PRAGUE

For a thousand years
stories have been told in Prague,
magical, mysterious, romantic legends,
stories of love and adventure...

Here you can read of old Bohemian rulers and artists, rich
men of Prague and its poor, the renowned buildings of
the ancient city, the loves of its people, their moments of
happiness and of suffering. The fate of the Czech nation
is reflected in the legends wreathing the capital city of
the Bohemian kingdom. This selective choice of the most
attractive Prague stories will be your guide on your walks
through Prague.

JAN VANIS:
A GUIDE TO MYSTERIOUS PRAGUE

This book is the first ever guide to the world of the Prague
ghosts, wraiths and phantoms – it can make your strolls
through Prague's nooks and corners exciting. It also has
a map on which you can find the haunts of Prague's weird
ghosts...

Eduard Petiška (1924–1987) is one of the best-known Czech writers. He is the author of numerous works both for the adult and young reader. Many of his seventy books met with a wide international acceptance. They have been translated into 27 languages and published in hundreds of editions abroad. The number of copies of Petiška's books has exceeded 10 million. "A Treasury of Tales from the Kingdom of Bohemia" ranks among the author's books devoted to myths and legends. In this group there appeared the legends of ancient Israel, Greece, Egypt and Mesopotamia, the stories of "A Thousand And One Nights" and a two volume book of legends from Bohemia, Moravia and Silesia.

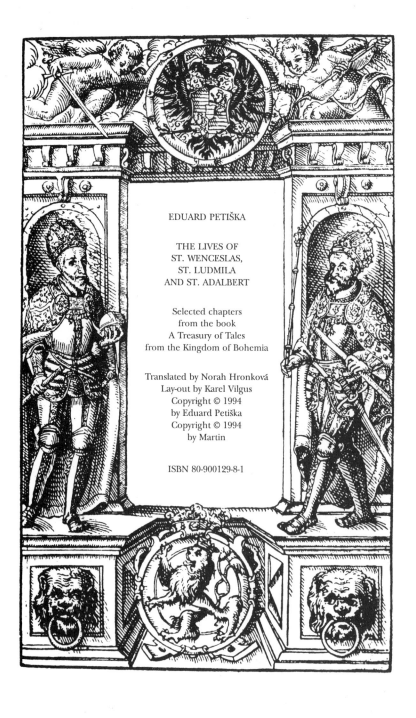

EDUARD PETIŠKA

THE LIVES OF
ST. WENCESLAS,
ST. LUDMILA
AND ST. ADALBERT

Selected chapters
from the book
A Treasury of Tales
from the Kingdom of Bohemia

Translated by Norah Hronková
Lay-out by Karel Vilgus
Copyright © 1994
by Eduard Petiška
Copyright © 1994
by Martin

ISBN 80-900129-8-1